A Pilgrimage to Luther's Germany

With HERBERT BROKERING
and ROLAND BAINTON

WINSTON PRESS

Portions of this book are excerpted
from *Here I Stand* by Roland H. Bainton,
copyright renewal © 1978
by Roland H. Bainton; used by permission of the
publisher, Abingdon Press.

The excerpts from
Here I Stand appear on the left
hand pages throughout this book.

Design and Art Production
by VISTA III DESIGN

Library of Congress Catalog Card Number: 82-51159
ISBN: 0-86683-629-2

Winston Press, Inc.   430 Oak Grove   Minneapolis, MN 55403

FOREWORD

The world holds the life and work of Martin Luther in high esteem. The Reformation released an enormous new energy into all levels of life. What Martin Luther did for all spheres of human existence is understood best, perhaps, by the beloved Luther scholar Dr. Roland Bainton. He has been a primary agent in uncovering the way Luther felt and thought, and in relating Luther's spiritual pilgrimage to the continuing journey of the whole human family.

Martin Luther's word and work are studied and admired in all walks of life. His life has inspired millions, in matters of faith, language, culture, education, art, music, family, society, labor, vocation, politics. Through the ages Luther has given theology a heartbeat that has not lost its rhythm or power in these five hundred years since his birth. Then — as today — faith and life, word and work are intricately and vividly interwoven.

A Pilgrimage to Luther's Germany weaves history, free verse, and photography into a pilgrimage for all walks of life. The signposts for a twentieth-century pilgrimage are partly in the texts, often in the images, and most of all in the reader's imagination. Deep inside us all, where our spiritual journey is renewed daily, stands the never-ending question: Who am I, and who am I to God?

Herbert Brokering

Did we in our own strength confide, Our striving would be losing, Were not the right man on our side, The man of God's own choosing. Dost ask who that may be? Christ Jesus, it is he; Lord Sabaoth his name. From age to age the same, And he must win the battle.

Martin Luther
From "A Mighty Fortress" Verse 2

Portrait of Luther by Lucas Cranach, a contemporary of Luther.

The woods came down to the fringes of the village to be continued by orchards and vineyards . . . with plantings of indigo, blue flowered flax, and yellow saffron; and nestling within the brilliant rows lay the walls, the gates, the steeples of many-spired Erfurt. Luther called her a new Bethlehem.

This man was no son of the Italian Renaissance, but a German born in remote Thuringia, where men of piety still reared churches with arches and spires straining after the illimitable. Luther was himself so much a gothic figure that his faith may be called the last great flowering of the religion of the Middle Ages.

When driven to the edge of existence in a bondage of castles and peasant slavery a religious disquiet will stir the human spirit to whisper: *Lord have mercy,* or raise a shout of piety: *Who am I to God?*

In the midst of spires, processions, gnomes, mermaids, witches, prayers, captive demons, relics, castles, shouts of saints and peasants toiling in the belly of the earth, there is the need to raise the question of existence: *Who am I?*

For them (the peasants) the woods and winds and water were peopled by elves, gnomes, fairies, mermen and mermaids, sprites and witches. Sinister spirits would release storms, floods, and pestilence, and would seduce mankind to sin and melancholia.

From the beginning to the end the only secure course was to lay hold of every help the Church had to offer: sacraments, pilgrimages, indulgences, the intercession of the saints.

Theology is a spirit-filled pendulum ranging from God's hell to God's hope. Theology driven by fear and mercy at once is a timebomb in the soul. In the mixture of salvation and despair we look hungrily for the kingdom of heaven or to the safest of all places upon earth.

For some, safety is in the church of sacrament and gospel. For some, the safest place is in old places where life begins, in old haunts and thoughts of goblins, and tormented pools and roots in nature. The pendulum swings between storms of demons and sacraments. Security is somewhere along the arc of the pendulum.

11

 Luther knew perfectly well why youths should make themselves old and nobles should make themselves abased. This life is only a brief period of training for the life to come, where the saved will enjoy an eternity of bliss and the damned will suffer everlasting torment . . . All this will last forever. . . . These were the ideas on which Luther had been nurtured. There was nothing peculiar in his beliefs or his response save their intensity.

As he returned to school after a visit with his parents, sudden lightning struck him to earth. In that single flash he saw the denouement of the drama of existence.

To the monastery he went like others, and even more than others, in order to make his peace with God.

The Augustinian cloister in Erfurt, where Luther became a monk.

Revelation of peace is fraction of time away and arises inside storms and whirlwinds. We can be saved in the worst of times as we are reconciled, on a pilgrimage where peacemaking is a glad journey into eventide or a struggle behind some locked door with God, one on one.

He was content to spend his days in prayer, in song, in meditation and quiet companionship, in disciplined and moderate austerity. Thus he might have continued had he not been overtaken by another thunderstorm, this time of spirit. The occasion was the saying of his first mass.

He related afterward: "I thought to myself, 'With what tongue shall I address such Majesty, seeing that all men ought to tremble in the presence of even an earthly prince? Who am I, that I should lift up mine eyes or raise my hands to the divine Majesty? . . .' "

Glory is overpowering; wonder overwhelming. The soul can cringe at the tolling of bells and be far too near for a trembling heart to hear. Some nights we see only from afar and the distant is near enough. We shield our blurry eyes before glory and look hopefully with shepherds and multitudes through windows which fracture the light and darkness into a miracle of mystery, and we bow heads.

The mere sight of a crucifix was to Luther like a stroke of lightning. He would flee, then, from the angry Son of the merciful Mother. He would appeal to the saints — twenty-one of them he had selected as his special patrons, three for each day of the week. All to no avail, for of what use is any intercession if God remains angry?

The All Terrible is the All Merciful too. Wrath and love fuse upon the cross.

How amazing that God in Christ . . . should be the All Loving too; that the ineffable Majesty should stoop to take upon himself our flesh, subject to hunger, cold, death and desperation. We see him lying in the feedbox of a donkey, laboring in the carpenter's shop, dying a derelict under the sin of the world. The gospel is not so much a miracle as a marvel, and every line is suffused with wonder.

*Symbols flourish in every corner,
upon every wall, to unveil fear and
faith at once. The cross absorbs all
terror till we are left with the sure
surprise of God in human spaces. Ah
the wonder of the common and of
warmth of holy ones inside a lean-to
shed. The spirit is quiet in the
soothing hush of gospel present in
places of work and daily bread.*

God is not praised if He is not loved; He is not loved if He does not do good; He does not do good if He is not gracious; He neither is nor can be gracious if He does not forgive sins; and He does not forgive sins except for Christ's sake.

Martin Luther

The tower of the Castle Church in Wittenberg.

The doors of the Castle Church in Wittenberg now cast in bronze with Luther's 95 theses inscribed on them.

Luther's new insights contained already the marrow of his mature theology.

The center about which all the petals clustered was the affirmation of the forgiveness of sins through the utterly unmerited grace of God made possible by the cross of Christ, which reconciled wrath with mercy.

Luther's Theses differed from the ordinary propositions for debate because they were forged in anger.

Luther took no steps to spread his theses among the people. He was merely inviting scholars to dispute and dignitaries to define, but others surreptitiously translated the theses into German and gave them to the press.

Emotions matter. Outrage can forge a
    revival.
A fire can reform an iron mountain.
A holy spirit can reform a people.
Reform is not simply personal; it is
    communal.
Compassion lifts a reformer's heart and
    nerve and energy for all the people.
In due time truth spreads like a flurry of
    gossip across a countryside.

A true witness does not spare conviction.
A true cause stakes life and death.
Rights of God or children cannot be
    usurped by any power of state or
    church.
Reform begins with a bold pen.
It throws all writings against Satan, and
    ends with the fiery wind of Pentecost.

German nationalism . . . was itself inchoate in Luther's day because Germany was retarded in national unification as compared with Spain, France, and England. Germany had no centralized government.

No government and no class was able to weld Germany into one. . . . Germany was segmented into small and overlapping jurisdictions of princes and bishops.

When death lurks near, a nation will be reborn. All parts of one body will be bound by one mother tongue and one native land.

All count. All legacies of generations flow and fit into one gigantic puzzle. Self respect is the bonding power of new people mothered with a common self esteem and tongue. A mystical depth in a soul can be tapped. When people have trembled before God they can be fearless before one another. The awakening of nation is a spiritual birthquake.

Luther was not concerned to philosophize about the structure of Church and state; his insistence was simply that every man must answer for himself to God.

Birth for him was not so isolated as death. One cannot die for another, but one can in a sense be initiated for another into a Christian community. For that reason baptism rather than the Lord's Supper is the sacrament which links the Church to society. It is the sociological sacrament.

"The temporal authorities are baptized with the same baptism as we." This is the language of the Christian society, built upon the sociological sacrament administered to every babe born into the community. In such a society, Church and state are mutually responsible for the support and correction of each other.

Rebirth is a wellspring and taps life at
　　its source — belonging.
We belong inside a network, fabric,
　　labyrinth, society, a sacramental
　　matrix.
Life is a community event.
Society is a festival of human cultures
　　in desperate, daily need of
　　wellbeing.

Through liturgies of birth and rebirth
　　a call resounds alike for priest and
　　politician, for church and state, to
　　form a human network — a pond.
There is a font for every marketplace,
　　a bursting symbol of belonging to
　　a holy catholic universe.

Luther resolved to make a trip incognito to Wittenberg. . . .

On Christmas Day 2,000 people assembled in the Castle Church — "the whole town," said a chronicler. And it very nearly was, for the total population was only 2,500.

Festivals of wellness are instantaneous. When the true word is told, crowds gather on their own. A world will migrate unannounced to meet when life is struck hard without warning or when a child of God is expected. Sometimes we go quick to see a great light, to stand in the midst of great faith and to quicken the night with candlelight.

The primary consideration with him was always the pre-eminence of religion. . . .
Luther would never shirk a mundane task such as exhorting the elector to repair
the city wall to keep the peasants' pigs from rooting in the villagers' gardens, but
he was never supremely concerned about pigs, gardens, walls, cities, princes, or
any and all of the blessings and nuisances of this mortal life. The ultimate problem
was always God and man's relationship to God.

The way to the cathedral is through the field, cafes, a cattle stall and the red-hot foundries. Everything that bellows, brays, coos and bows is in the narthex of the nave. The ordinary ushers in the holy until we are in such a place we cannot stand without a shawl for shading down of eyes and face. The more human the journey the more holy. The soul steps high and careful through pig sty and courtyard on the determined way to see God. All life is accountable as one voice to the One who is at once center and circumference of immortality.

Luther's answer is that mortality must be grounded somewhere else than in self-help and the quest for reward. The paradox is that God must destroy in us all illusions of righteousness before he can make us righteous. First we must relinquish all claim of goodness. The way to eliminate feelings of guilt is to admit guilt. Then there is some hope for us. "We are sinners and at the same time righteous " — which is to say that however bad we are, there is a power at work in us which can and will make something of us.

The dynamic of the human spirit is a spiral force, a whirlwind, and in its quiet center a flame of faith is fearless, faithful, fervent, full. Redemption is the tug in force fields of sin and grace, saint and sinner.

There is a flood of power unleashed through us, surging silently from realms deeper than the inner brain, and its fire lights on us and in us. All fire is a great combustion.

Just as our neighbor suffers want and is in need of our surplus, so we have suffered want before God and were in need of His grace. Therefore as God has helped us freely through Christ, so we should devote our body and its activities to helping our neighbor.

Martin Luther

German countryside as seen from the top of Wartburg Castle.

As there is no need to tell lovers what to do and say, so there is no need for any rules to those who are in love with Christ. The only word that covers all this is faith.

This is the word which ought to be placarded as the epitome of Luther's ethic, that a Christian must be a Christ to his neighbor.

Christ is in the neighborhood.
Christ is host and guest of every household.

Faith bows and bends us like good shepherds
    tending newfound lambs rejoicing.
Faith bends knees in Bethlehem and
    San Francisco.
The Spirit's fruit is faith,
and faith has eyes for Christ in every
    neighborhood.

The gospel could be exemplified only in the midst of secular callings, except that Luther refused to call them secular.

As he extended the priesthood to all believers, so likewise he extended the concept of divine calling, vocation, to all worthy occupations.

Our expression "vocational guidance" comes directly from Luther. God has called men to labor because he labors. He works at common occupations. God is a tailor who makes for the deer a coat that will last for a thousand years. He is a shoemaker who provides boots that the deer will not outlive. God is a butler who sets forth a feast for the sparrows and spends on them annually more than the revenue of the king of France. Christ came as a carpenter.

No work is too common for good or God's glory. God is at work in bread, through milk and under word and water. All earth belongs to God and all who plant it, turn it, pluck it, sing it, eat it. We take the harvest from the hand of God with awe.

So labor is for all a work of faith and wonder. God who tells the storm be still calls for raspberries to ripen and just laws to pass. So it has been from the beginning and it is very good to still be so.

The demarcation of the
spheres of Church and state
correspond in a rough way to
dualisms running through
the nature of God and man.
God is wrath and mercy. The
state is the instrument of his
wrath, the Church of his
mercy. Man is divided into
outward and inward. Crime
is outward and belongs to the
state. Sin is inward and
belongs to the Church.
Goods are outward and fall
to the state. Faith is inward
and falls to the Church.

The magistrate has his
calling; the minister his
calling. Each must serve God
according to his office. One
calling is not better than
another. One is not easier
than another. There are
temptations peculiar to each.

Both doors are home and
　　both give welcome.
One gives us civil rights, the
　　other virtues.
From one we go to campaign
　　for all rights and duties.
From the other we go
　　endowed, renewed,
　　blessed, strengthened.
God has two doors.
There is the door for flesh;
　　there is the door for spirit.
Two doors for everyone.
Each is under call, and every
　　calling is in danger.
Together all do service before
　　God, priest and princess.

But the spirit of work should not be grim. Let the birds here teach us a lesson. If you say, "Hey, birdie, why are you so gay? You have no cook, no cellar," he will answer, "I do not sow, I do not reap, I do not gather into barns. But I have a cook, and his name is Heavenly Father. . . ."

When you suffer, wrap it in a melody.
When you fear, whisper it to a migrant
    wren.
When you dread, confess it to a lily of
    the field.

Learn of nature how to sing.
Sing! What words are left for fear?
Sing! What pain is left to curse?
Sing! Half of all the angels sing.
Sing! All Cherubim still sing.
Sing! All Seraphim still serve.
Rejoice and obey.

Luther is at his best and most characteristic in his sermons on the Nativity.

"There are many of you in this congregation who think to yourselves: "If only I had been there! How quick I would have been to help the Baby! I would have washed his linen. How happy I would have been to go with the shepherds to see the Lord lying in the manger!" Yes, you would! You say that because you know how great Christ is, but if you had been there at that time you would have done no better than the people of Bethlehem. . . . Why don't you do it now? You have Christ in your neighbor.

Christ is not confined inside a nation's holiday, nor in the grandeur of a cherished holy day. There are signs of Christ among the masses, midst two or three going in the name of Jesus, traveling cross-country with attache cases and lunch boxes, riding, passing, waving, flying, walking, *honking. In the meeting of another is the miracle. All such simple signs of God's real presence confounds our wisdom and depression. The great embarrassment and reassurance is this: Christ is even here and never leaves us.*

43

God lays souls into the lap of married people, souls begotten from their own body, on which they may practice all Christian works. For when they teach their children the Gospel, parents are certainly their apostles, bishops, and ministers.

Martin Luther

The door to Luther's house in Wittenberg.

On the appointed day at ten o'clock in the morning Luther led Katherine to the sound of bells through the streets of Wittenberg to the parish church, where at the portal in the sight of all the people the religious ceremony was observed.

Of course the Christian should love his wife, said Luther. He is bound to love his neighbor as himself. His wife is his nearest neighbor. Therefore she should be his dearest friend.

He paid her the highest tribute when he called St. Paul's epistle to the Galatians "my Katherine von Bora." He began to be a trifle worried over his devotion: "I give more credit to Katherine than to Christ, who has done so much more for me."

*Love cannot be purchased and is without
   price.*
Love blushes poor and rich alike.
*Love shines more priceless than a
   treasure.*
Love survives old age.
A true lover will sometimes rival God.

The whole institution of marriage was set by Luther within the framework of family relationship. There was no room left for the exercise of unbridled individualism.

Luther thoroughly enjoyed his home. Once his colleague Jonas remarked that he saw the blessing of God in fruit and for that reason had hung a cherry bough above his table. Luther said, "Why don't you think of your children? They are in front of you all the time, and you will learn from them more than from a cherry bough."

Luther reveled in household festivities and may well have composed for Hans and Lenchen the Christmas pageant Von Himmel Hoch with its delightful, childlike quality. Equally charming is this brief carol:

What the globe could not
   enwrap
Nestled lies in Mary's lap.
Just a baby, very wee,
Yet Lord of the world is
   he.

*Every age must face with some
amazement unwrapping gifts of God,
unveiling King of Kings in lap of
peasant girl, and claiming sure the
child is ours. Every age must spring
with joy before the paradox: the All
in All a baby wee.*

*What philosophy can fathom: the
only Son our Lord cradled in a crib of
hay, the everlasting God outside a
holy city pouring out with pity
through his tears. Every generation is
blessed to stare in faith to face
nativity eye to eye.*

The church is the pupil of Christ, sitting at His feet and hearing His Word so that she may know how to pass judgment on everything, how to serve in one's calling, how to administer public offices, aye, also how to eat, drink, and sleep, that there may be no doubt about the proper conduct in any walk of life but, surrounded on all sides by the Word of God, one may constantly walk in joy and in the light.

Martin Luther

Luther's pulpit in the Wittenberg Church.

Christian princes in his view were certainly responsible for fostering the true religion. Luther's concern was always that the faith be unimpeded. Anyone might help; no one might hinder.

Luther was above all else a man of prayer, and yet of his prayers we have less than of his sermons and conversations because he succeeded in keeping his students out of the secret chamber. . . . Give us graciously thy peace and spare us from war. Grant to our Kaiser wisdom and understanding that he may govern his earthly kingdom in peace and blessedness. Give to all kings, princes, and lords good counsel that they may direct their lands in quietness and justice.

The mayor may light the fire of the acolyte whose altar candles flicker against shop windows and beckon executives and clerks to tell the truth. High cathedral keeps watch over downtown, for those who kneel to drink are those who sell. God's crucifix emerges painfully out of any mold of bronze or stone or human flesh. Christ reappears through hot-cross buns or barbed wire to confess again: It is I against whom you kick and goad.

Memorial to the dead at Dachau.

The true Christian Church is the work of the Word communicated by every available means. Early Luther sensed the need for a new translation of the Scriptures from the original tongues into idiomatic German. There must be likewise a body of instructional material for the young.

Liturgy would have to be revised . . . to enlighten the people. Congregational singing should be cultivated alike to inspire and instruct. The Bible, the catechism, the liturgy, and the hymnbook thus constituted the needs, and all four were to be met by Luther himself.

Liturgy orchestrates all life into a mission of learning life with wonder. Revelation is clothed in chasubles and chancels and company dress codes and checkered smocks of red and white. Revelation threads the liturgical walk which is the pilgrimage from ever into ever. Liturgy is the human motion of everyone enroute expecting that all which breaks be lifted up as holy. The Word of God is broken into its many parts.

For the translation of the Bible, Luther availed himself of the enforced leisure at the Wartburg to produce in three months a rendering of the complete New Testament. . . . For the German, Luther's rendering was incomparable. He leaped beyond the tradition of a thousand years. . . . There had been translations before him . . . . But none had the majestic diction, the sweep of vocabulary, the native earthiness, and the religious profundity of Luther.

Luther insisted that the idiom of one language must be translated into the equivalent of the other. He was scornful of the Vulgate translation, "Hail, Mary, full of grace." . . . I would prefer to say simply, 'Liebe Maria'.

The Wartburg Castle.

Language is a living work. The Spirit hovers over all true stories to shape the Scriptures with the people. The Word is original in every tongue. Every people, culture, age and kind translate into mother tongue, and look for accents, paraphrases, dialects and mental pictures. The life of Christ is alive and well. Life is the kernel in every tough text.

The Bible, just as it stood in Luther's rendering, was a great educational tool; but more was needed, obviously for children, but also for adults, who were almost equally ignorant. . . . Hence Luther's plea for municipal schools with a system of compulsory education including religion. . . . "The Scripture cannot be understood without the languages . . . and the languages can be learned only in school."

The whole tone of the service was altered in two respects: there was more of the scriptural and more of the instructional. . . . The church thus became not only the house of prayer and praise but also a classroom.

We ask and answer together.
God and we are on one
learning log in dialogue.
Learning is enlightenment,
sanctifying.
Faith will not forfeit
knowing and perceiving.
Understanding and
appreciating is not a
human option.
We mark main themes in
magic yellow.

Catechizing is the Word and
world in conversation.
Each will ask the other for
the answer.
Conversing is the format for
the journey.
Talking is the rule of every
catechism.
What does it mean to me, to
you, to us, to God?

The Reformation gave centrality to the sermon. The pulpit was higher than the altar, for Luther held that salvation is through the Word and without the Word the elements are devoid of sacramental quality, but the Word is sterile unless spoken.

His pre-eminence in the pulpit derives in part from the earnestness with which he regarded the preaching office. The task of the minister is to expound the Word, in which alone are to be found healing for life's hurts and the balm of eternal blessedness. The preacher must die daily through concern lest he lead his flock astray.

Go tell it! The Word of God is force, a stream of consciousness, a living river. The Word of God is the power for breaking open the grave, and for the right distribution of all property. The Word will break the silence of our sinning.

Can the Word lose its swift speed? A river can run dry. A spring can disappear. The Word will route water into a lengthy journey. In the beginning was the Word, a sound without end. The pulpit is the place to hear this great sound and to see the stilling of every raging sea. Hear the Word, take off shoes, and see the burning bush. The pulpit is the watch-tower, the high ground in flood times. The Gospel is the force of salvation.

For if you want to revive the sad, startle the jovial, encourage the despairing, humble the conceited, pacify the raving, mollify the hate-filled — and who is able to enumerate all the lords of the human heart, I mean the emotions of the heart and the urges which incite a man to all virtues and vices? — what can you find that is more efficacious than music?

Martin Luther

The Luther Bibles were copiously illustrated, particularly for the earlier portion of the Old Testament and for the book of Revelation in the New Testament. . . . Within the conventional limits Luther's Bible was richly illustrated. In the various editions to appear during his lifetime there were some five-hundred woodcuts. They were not the choicest expressions of the art, but they did Germanize the Bible.

Every culture paints its pride and pain
into the backdrop of the Word, and
casts the cross in clay or oil or bronze
and does so all by heart — an
original. Children with their dolls and
finger plays, and motion choirs all in
white exhibit their original of Jesus,
on the spot, in Nazareth, in Erfurt,
downtown, uptown, across town. The
text will seek its total context.
Incarnation is a phenomenon of God
among us and we behold glory in
regional color tones. The Word of
God is an endless unfolding of sights.

"Next after theology I give to music the highest place and the greatest honor."

". . . With all my heart I extol the precious gift of God in the noble art of music, but I scarcely know where to begin or end. There is nothing on earth which has not its tone. Even the air invisible sings when smitten with a staff. Among the beasts and the birds song is still more marvelous. . . . Music is to be praised as second only to the Word of God because by her are all the emotions swayed.

The last and greatest reform of all was in the congregational song. . . . Luther so developed this element that he may be considered the father of congregational song. This was the point at which his doctrine of the priesthood of all believers received its most concrete realization.

Music is the servant of theology, the handmaid of the Lord.
Music cradles newest thoughts and rhymes our doctrine.
Music strains to hold all paradoxes in balance and turns concepts into fugues and Bach chorales.
Music makes the way for rainy dirges, spirit dancing, and keeps the heart from falling. To know God is first prize.
Music, then, is second.
Music is the metronome upon the pilgrimage.

Luther's room in his home in Wittenberg.

Just when you feel that temptation is strongest and you are most unprepared to pray, then go to a place where you are alone, and pray the Lord's Prayer and whatever you can possibly say against Satan and his temptation. Then you will feel that the temptation becomes less severe and that Satan takes flight.

Martin Luther

Luther's whole life was a struggle against them [depressions], a fight for faith. This is the point at which he interests us so acutely, for we too are cast down and we too would know how to assuage our despondency.

The first comfort which he offered was the reflection that intense upheavals of the spirit are necessary for valid solutions of genuine religious problems. The emotional reactions may be unduly acute, for the Devil always turns a louse into a camel. Nevertheless the way of man with God cannot be tranquil.

Luther attached great importance to his baptism. When the devil assailed him, he would answer, "I am baptized."

Another good way, counseled Luther, to exorcize the Devil is to harness the horse and spread manure on the fields.

Statue of
Dietrich Bonhoeffer,
saint and martyr.

We wrestle from birth against princes
    and peasants who have lost sight of
    the neighbor.
Every seed struggles to keep its own
    life in death.
The Spirit calms the tempted and
    casts out fear of all in battle.
The God of hosts has met the foe
    inside the font.

Remember the baptism.
Remember the victor at the fountain
    where the first flood was
    transformed into a covenant.
Get behind me, Satan, I am baptized.
Be still, dear heart, the fight is won.

. . . if God hides himself in the storm clouds which brood over the brow of Sinai, then gather about the manger, look upon the infant Jesus as he leaps in the lap of his mother, and know that the hope of the world is here.

Or again, if Christ and God alike are unapproachable, then look upon the firmament of the heavens and marvel at the work of God, who sustains them without pillars. Or take the meanest flower and see in the smallest petals the handiwork of God.

The creche nestles at the foothills of
Sinai, and is a resting place for pilgrims
tired by the climb. Hope is in the one in
the lap, whose power is stronger than the
roots of old commandments. We too
cradle counselors, martyrs and princes of
peace. We too plant shrubs and tulips
and monuments that magnify the Lord.

See the tiniest blossom, and in the petal
is a handiwork for fingers finer than
needlepoint. The God who shaped high
seas and massed star galaxies has knitted
us inside a womb in a microscopic
beginning. A child in the lap is most
nearly the Word of God.

If one would discover parallels to Luther as the wrestler with the Lord, then one must turn to Paul the Jew, Augustine the Latin, Pascal the Frenchman, Kierkegaard the Dane, Unamuno the Spaniard, Dostoevski the Russian, Bunyan the Englishman, and Edwards the American.

In his religion he was Hebrew, not a Greek fancying gods and goddesses disporting themselves about some limpid pool or banqueting upon Olympus. The God of Luther, as of Moses, was the God who inhabits the storm clouds and rides on the wings of the wind. At his nod the earth trembles, and the people before him are as a drop in the bucket. . . . Yet the All Terrible is the All Merciful too. . . . How shall we know this? In Christ, only in Christ.

All may share in the legacy of Luther.
All sometimes frozen in cold terror can
   be comforted, in Christ.
All who face a high wall of an
   omnipotent God can find the
   doorway, in Christ.

In Christ all terror is tamed in native
   tongue.
In Christ the Lord of Lords befriends a
   monk in Wittenberg.
In Christ justice is a neighbor away.
In Christ a scientific finding is the
   offering.

In Christ the Scriptures open life to
   wholeness.
In Christ the princess and the peasant are
   both priest.
In Christ all life is gift and all are
   beggars.

God help us as He has helped our ancestors and will also help our descendents to the praise and honor of His divine name throughout eternity! For we are, after all, not the sort of people who could sustain the church. Nor were our forefathers; nor will our descendents be such. But the Lord has done it, is doing it now, and will do it. He says, "I am with you unto the end of the world."